THE ULTIMATE GUIDE TO
LIST & SELL
COMMERCIAL INVESTMENT PROPERTY

BY

MICHAEL SIMPSON

TheNCREA
THE NATIONAL COMMERCIAL REAL ESTATE ASSOCIATION

Published in Long Beach, California by The National Commercial Real
Estate Association

www.theNCREA.com

Photography by Square Line Photography
www.SquarelinePhotography.com

ISBN: 978-1978228443

Make your day count.

CONTENTS

ACKNOWLEDGMENTS

Nobody succeeds alone. There are so many people I want to thank! Where to start? Reflecting back, I have found writing this to be a challenge. I have learned so much from so many people.

One of the first who comes to mind is Mic Craven, my high school track coach. He taught me how to "remove myself from myself" so as not to feel the pain in my body, which helps when you try to push yourself higher than you think is possible. I thank my grandparents. They helped me pursue my dreams. Because of them, I found the courage to move from Oregon to California as a kid right out of high school.

Another person who has meant a lot to me was my first broker, Vicki Mullins. She convinced me to hang in there and stay in real estate when I was ready to quit. I also want to thank Sindy Verdugo, a top agent, who took me under her wing my first year in Real Estate and mentored me in learning the ropes.

The Mike Ferry Organization helped me learn to treat my business *as* a business, which allowed me to grow to over 100 plus transactions a year.

Del Wall, my first commercial mentor, taught me so much! He taught me what I call the Grid System, along with several other first-class strategies for investment real estate. Erica Hill, an entrepreneur and Keller Williams Regional Owner, Franchise Owner and Business Partner who taught me "The hard gets easy, or the easy gets hard."

Gary Keller, the founder of Keller Williams, taught me the power of systems and the power in delegating. Most importantly, he encouraged me to pursue my dreams and passions to create the life I wanted.

James Malinchak, who is a coach for Public Speakers who teaches the business side of speaking, opened my eyes to the vision and possibilities involved with speaking, training, and coaching. Training and coaching have been a dream come true for me, even though I went for years without knowing that these are the things I most wanted to do in life.

Jamey and Joey Bridges coached me for several years. They helped my entire team understand and learn the systems necessary to operate a multi-million-dollar training company, and they have been instrumental in staying on my butt to get this book done! I also want to thank Todd Bates (R.I.P.). He taught me to simplify and focus on what matters.

To my first coaching members, Rima Rafeh and Kory Jackson, thank you for jumping in when I asked you, and for having faith in me! You got our coaching program off the ground by allowing me to share your massive success stories!

Dena Edgmon, my Customer Service and East Coast Operations Manager, deserves a lot of credit for helping me run this great company.

Steven Moraldo, my nephew, he is a Marine and an inspiration to me. Steven constantly shares his stories of working with me in the past. He suggested that I add some of my history to this book.

A key and important person in my life is Kelley Fischer, my loving and loyal friend and assistant who stayed by my side through thick and thin for 15 years.

Everyone thanks their mom, right? Well, I'm no different. My Mom (who is now in heaven R.I.P.) taught me to always do the right thing, always be persistent and to live a life of integrity.

My daughter and dive buddy, Bethany, has put up with me not being as available as we would have liked over the years. She will always be "My Goose."

Last, and certainly not least, my lovely wife, Angie Simpson. Angie got my mind working. It was through her encouragement and support that I even got into the real estate business in the first place. Angie was in college and I studied Real Estate. She carried me financially, and has always been my #1 raving fan. Love you, Babe! Thank you!

Of course, if it were not for the faith and belief of all my students, coaching members, team leaders, operating partners, managers, brokers, education coordinators, and everyone who has given me a shot at a speaking event, and who became raving fans, none of this would be happening today. You all are the best! Honestly, I have many more people to thank for my success in life. You know who you are, and I know there will be more good times to come!

INTRODUCTION

I showed the manuscript of this book to my nephew when I thought it was finished. He has worked with me at times, so he knows what it took for me to build my real estate career. He told me he liked the book, but suggested that I share with you how I went from zero earnings in the first 12 months to where I am now. My initial reaction was that no one outside the family would be interested in my story. Then I reconsidered.

As the founder and senior instructor of The National Commercial Real Estate Association (The NCREA), I have more than 27 years of experience and bring first-hand knowledge to agents and investors who want to learn how to make money in the commercial and investment industry.

I am an independent broker who has owned several Keller Williams franchises and have been affiliated with RE/MAX and Century 21. My training, consulting, and coaching company combines real-world strategies with university-style training.

My credentials include:

- *Being in the Top one percent of all agents in the US*
- *Top three commercial agents - California/Hawaii*
- *Consistently averaged more than 50 sales per year*
- *National Commercial Real Estate Advisor (NCREA)*
- *Certified Real Estate Investment Planning Specialist, (C.R.E.I.P.S.)*
- *REO & Short Sale Specialist*
- *Past Director California Association of Realtors (CAR)*
- *Past Director and Arbitrator for Pacific West Association of Realtors (PWR), the fifth largest board in nation*
- *Arbitrator for California Association of Realtors & Pacific West Association of Realtors*

More than once, someone has asked me to "write a book," so here it is. At The NCREA, I teach an one-day training course for residential agents who want to learn how to do commercial deals. This book grew out of that training. It's an introductory book written for residential agents just starting to work in the commercial industry, but experienced commercial Realtors will also find valuable information for growing their businesses.

I teach from personal experience, which is why I can assure you that my methods work. I decided to tell my story in hope that you'll realize I'm a regular person just like you. My success isn't because of an outstanding personality, although that can help, and it isn't because I have natural charm, although my wife sometimes says that I do. I tell you in all honesty that my success has come from the mentoring and training I've received, along with the fact that I applied what I have learned. You can experience the same success if you're willing to learn and put in the work. And if, like me, you just keep at it.

In this book, and the accompanying workbook, I've attempted to include everything that you need to become a success in commercial real estate. If you still need help, do not hesitate to contact me. I will be glad to offer recommendations or help you find solutions to problems.

If you ask for help, be aware that my mentoring style is not to just give you the answer. My style is to help you figure out the answer. That is the best way to learn. I am committed to your ongoing learning and success as a commercial/investment agent. You can contact me via:

🌐 www.TheNCREA.com

✉ info@TheNCREA.com

📞 877-877-1543

f /TheNationalCommercialRealEstateAssociation

 /c/michaelsimpsonthencrea

The purpose of Life should
be to pursue your Passions.
The purpose of Business should
be to fund that Purpose.

~ Michael Simpson

CHAPTER 1

MY STORY

In 1988, I was a young guy living in Long Beach, California. I worked at an aerospace company near the airport (LAX) as a Non-Destructive Testing (NDT) Inspector, which was a fun skill I'd learned to do underwater in dive school, although it was a different experience doing it top-side.

The money was good, but I didn't like the job. The truth is, I hated the job, but it didn't bother me much because I spent most of my time watching sports and chasing girls. The job paid the bills, and life was good.

Then everything changed. I met someone who I knew was "the one." Life got even better, but not long into our relationship, my girlfriend asked me what I intended to do when I grew up. Yikes! Talk about pressure. Worse still, I knew she had a point.

The problem was I had absolutely no idea. Yeah, I know, but I'm being honest here. I didn't have a career dream.

I didn't even have a vague idea of what I might like to do, other than, of course, I wanted things to work out with my girlfriend.

One Saturday I locked myself in my shared house, determined to come up with a plan or at least a direction. The day dragged on and nothing, and I mean nothing, came to me. I was stuck.

Then fate came calling. Late one afternoon, someone knocked on my door. A guy standing on the other side, Bill Miller, said he managed a local real estate company. He asked if I would be interested in buying something. I told him no. Then he asked if I'd like to work at his office.

Strange as it might sound, I had only one thought: This is it! I'd locked myself in my house that day determined that I wouldn't leave until I had a plan. And then, the knock on the door. Without hesitating, I told the guy yes.

Long story short, I kept working at the aerospace company during the day, and after work, I drove an hour south to Long Beach, which is where I lived and where the real estate office was. I did cold calling at the real estate office from 5:00 pm - 8:30 pm. If you saw the movie Glengarry Glenn Ross (a great movie, if you haven't seen it), you know what my life was like. I did straight cold calling out of a book you might be familiar with, The Haines Criss+Cross Directory, and got a lot of nothing from my efforts.

Little did I know, but fate had stepped into my life in another way. I was fortunate to have landed at a real estate office that focused on listings. The entire office was pretty much all about listings and farming. Looking back now, I'm grateful for that because it taught me the valuable lesson of "list-to-last." Remember that. We are going to talk a lot about listings in this book because you'll find that your real estate business will be sustainable if you can supply it with a steady stream of listings. We'll talk about how to do that using the systems I teach. More about that later.

As you might guess, I struggled in the first months of my part-time real estate work. Who wouldn't? It took time to get the hang of cold calling. Plus, I'd signed up for some real estate classes. Between a full-time job, a part-time job, and the classes, I was a whirlwind of activity.

What helped me most during those early months was that the broker and the agents in the office supported me, for which I'm still appreciative. Take that as a lesson for developing your career. Everyone needs help now and then. When you find people who are knowledgeable and willing to advise you, do all you can to learn from them.

So, night after night and week after week I kept calling, and I earned my license in 1989. Then, about six months into the cold calling, I got a listing appointment!

However, being a newbie, I blew the first step; I underpriced the listing. I figured out my mistake about two minutes after I posted the listing on the board when a slew of offers came in from the savvy agents in the office. Embarrassing, yes, the whole thing was very public and very embarrassing. I also had to go back to the seller with my manager, which was also embarrassing, but the seller appreciated our honesty. I am friends with that seller to this day.

That listing (and what I thought would be a related purchase) from this first client gave me the confidence, not to mention the expected revenue, to feel that I could take the leap and go into real estate full time.

Around this same time, my boss at the aerospace company called me in and said, "Simpson, we have good news and bad news. The good news is you're not laid off. We like your work ethic. The bad news is you're moving to the graveyard shift." Now that meant working from something like 11:30 p.m. to 7:00 a.m. And remember, I was completely involved with my smoking hot girlfriend and had a heavy duty social calendar!

So, with the dream of real estate success within my grasp, I told the aerospace company that real estate was what I loved, and, in a nice way, that they could take the aerospace job and shove it! Actually, it all worked out for the best. The area where the aerospace company was located is now a parking lot due to the industry taking a crash in the early 1990s.

Full-time Realtor now baby!
Super stoked! Then bam!

My real estate dream blew up in my face.

My lone client popped a bankruptcy and a tax lien on the FSBO they were buying (full three percent negotiated to represent buyer on that FSBO by yours truly), and I got hit with pretty much every other unexpected challenge a newbie who just quit his paying job could imagine.

I was stressed and did the only thing I could do, which was to work even harder. Luckily, once again I received help, this time from the number one agent in the office who got me going on a farm. My girlfriend and Mr. Visa helped me buy marketing materials, and I door knocked in that farm of 500 two times a month like there was no tomorrow!

At the time, total domination was all I thought about. I did it all: refrigerator magnets, calendars, pumpkins on Halloween, 4th of July flags, Easter plants, and extensive, heavy marketing with 24 Open House signs (branded the right way) every single weekend without fail.

I hired cheap labor like my young nephews to help me haul all this stuff around and distribute it, but even so, the money didn't last long. In no time, my girlfriend's money and Mr. Visa were maxed out. And I wasn't getting any new business. My one-year anniversary was coming up, and things didn't look like they were improving.

I had hit a wall. I didn't have a job that brought in any money, and now I was broke! On the day when I realized I couldn't keep going, I went into my broker's office about as defeated as a person can be. I told her that real estate was not for me, that I was out of money, and that I had to quit and find a paying job.

But I got lucky that day. My broker talked me into hanging in a little longer. She told me to focus on door knocking. After all, I didn't need funds for that. I will never forget her saying, "Stick to it. You're on the right track, Michael."

Were it not for her good advice at such a crucial time, I might not be in real estate today.

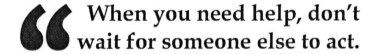 **When you need help, don't wait for someone else to act.**

When you find yourself in a tough spot, find a knowledgeable person and ask for support.

I stuck to it, and one month later --- month 12 ---boom! I got my first listing in the farm! Then boom, a buyer for that listing. Then another listing. By early 1990, I was the most talked about "overnight success" around!

However, it was not overnight. It was twelve months of intense learning and work. I ran full speed seven days a week and leveraged every dollar I could get my hands on before success found me!

With those first heart-stopping listings, I was finally making a living as a real estate agent. But I kept working just as hard to propel myself forward. I went to every training and seminar available and learned everything I could from people who were successful. I modeled hundreds of top agents across the country and implemented their systems.

Everywhere in this book, I stress the importance of training in building your career. I urge you to take advantage of every training opportunity.

By 1991, I had used the knowledge I'd gained to build a mega residential team. Perhaps I'll write another book about how that works. For now, I'll give you the short version. I built a team of five that included administrative support, buyer agents, telemarketers, and a transaction coordinator. Together, we hit 100 transactions per year for seven years! More good things happened during this time. Best of all, in 1992, my girlfriend and I got married. We'd studied together while she was in school at UCLA and I was learning the real estate business. She learned a lot about real estate just by listening to recordings I made of terminology and from my various classes. In fact, she later went on to get her license. At one point, I hired her as a team leader, but we learned it was better that we didn't work together. We do great as a couple, but not so great working together. I've often wondered how so many married couples work together in real estate.

Fast forward to 1998, when I happened to see a flyer for a class on commercial real estate. Remember, my mindset was always to be learning from as many successful people as I could. Yes, even though I was successful, I still took advantage of every available opportunity to learn from others.

The class turned out to be an intense one. For six months, I spent several hours a week working on that class. And guess what? I fell in love with commercial real estate and everything about it. What got me were the numbers and the fact that commercial real estate is more logical and less emotional than residential. Bottom line, you look at the numbers and either a deal makes sense or it doesn't.

After the class, the instructor asked me if I'd like to come to his office and help them build a commercial division. The office was in Los Alamitos, California, which was a nearby location, and the instructor offered to mentor me.

I thought, "Well, what a great opportunity!" I worked part- time at his office and helped build the commercial division. At the same time, I kept my residential business going. After all, that's where I was making money.

Just as important, and this is another key point, I started time blocking two hours a day for my commercial business. I'll talk more about time blocking in this book. It's fundamental to building and maintaining a successful real estate business.

Time blocking helped me plan my days and helped me stick to my two-hours-a-day commercial work schedule. But time blocking alone wasn't enough. I'd achieved success in residential, and I'd spent more time than I can tell you in classes and seminars learning how to work in the commercial world. With all of that, I thought I was good to go.

 As the Old Song Says, "I Did It My Way"

Are you expecting to read that I made money right away in commercial real estate? What happened was the opposite. Try as I might, I struggled, and the struggle went on for several months.

Why? Do you wonder if I was held back by something to do with commercial clients or maybe a lack of knowledge? It's accurate to say that I was juggling a lot of balls and managing a lot of change. Think about it. I still had my residential business going, and I'd hired my nephew to run it while I was starting my commercial business ---and I was burning through a lot of money.

At first, my nephew wasn't as experienced in running the residential business so we weren't making as much money. Plus, I was spending money on commercial marketing materials. But the main reason I struggled in those early months of working commercial/investment real estate was a simple one, although it took me several months to realize it.

When I first started in commercial real estate, I didn't follow the lead-generating system my mentor had taught me! Oh, I knew how to price commercial properties and how to calculate whether something was a good deal. But I burned through massive funds and wasted a lot of time because I was working my own lead generation methods instead of relying on the system I'd been trained to do.

Don't get me wrong. I'm not saying you can't invent your own way of doing something. If I'd been willing, or able, to put in the time and money required, I probably could have been successful eventually in "doing it my way." The problem was, which is the same problem for most of us, I didn't have that kind of time or money.

Not applying the system I'd been taught is where I went wrong and I didn't even realize it. I almost gave up. But before doing that, I asked my mentor for a heart-to-heart talk. I don't know what I expected from him, although I felt the need to tell him why I was quitting.

The first thing he asked me was what I thought I was doing, because what I was doing wasn't what he'd taught me. He came right out and said, "I didn't teach you to do any of the stuff you're doing." I looked at him and realized he was right.

It was like a cartoon where someone suddenly "gets" it. From then on, I started following the system he'd taught me. By making that one change, I turned things around. I'm going to teach you that same system in this book.

I call it the *Grid System*. It's a strategic way of looking at and managing your business, and one that no one who wants to fast-track their way to success can be without. There are other systems that I teach as well, but I consider The Grid "the gold!"

From the day I started doing what my mentor taught me to do, my commercial/investment business took off. With only two hours a day of my time, it paid me more than my residential business that was doing 100 transactions per year! I landed at number three in California and Hawaii for top commercial real estate agents.

Following my early success, I brought my nephew onto my team to manage my residential business, and I focused 100 percent of my time on my commercial/investment business. I learned a lot during this time. I became more polished in my approach. Sure, anyone will do that with experience, but I learned some other things as well. For example, I learned that it's more effective to consult than it is to sell.

In my early years as a commercial/investment agent, I thought I needed to sell myself, to convince potential clients that I was the best agent for the job. I soon learned that I needed to be a consultant, not a salesperson.

The reason is that clients don't always understand the possibilities available to them. Another issue is that clients don't always have a clear understanding of their goals or the best investment strategies to reach those goals.

When you consult, you educate clients without talking down to them. By doing this, you'll assist your clients in defining their specific goals and investment strategies. If you can learn to do that, you will achieve your goals.

In this same vein, I learned that it's not enough to just talk about goals and strategies. To be truly effective, you'll need to prepare written real estate investment plans for your clients. You need to be sure, so to speak, that you and your client are on the same page.

Things were going well for me, and then opportunity knocked again. I was introduced to a national franchise in 2002, and I opened franchises in Long Beach, Lakewood, and Los Alamitos, California, A top priority for me was to set up training for the agents in my offices.

Working with small groups of agents, I started teaching a spreadsheet method that I'd developed for obtaining and tracking my commercial transactions. Other people heard about the training and asked if I would come to their offices. I said, "Well, I'd never thought about that, but sure, okay!"

So I started traveling to other offices to do training and then it developed into teaching through Real Estate Board Associations, mainly in California. Then I moved into teaching in other states and into this awesome massive training, coaching, and consulting company we now have.

I still list and sell, and keep current with changes in the market, but my focus is on coaching and training residential agents who want to break into commercial real estate and investment sales, which I call *Resimercial*® real estate.

I can assure you that my success has come from applying the principles and systems I've been taught, along with the ones that I've developed over time, and then putting in the work. You can have the same success if you're willing to do the same.

Sure, I made mistakes along the way, and I expect that you will as well. But once I understood what I needed to do, I turned the tide and broke through to a successful career. You can do the same.

SUMMARY

L et's review the themes I've mentioned in my story. Keep them in mind as you read the book. Think about how you can apply these ideas to your business, and keep in mind that, like me, your success will build on itself.

1 Take advantage of training opportunities

Fundamental to your success will be your ability to learn and to keep learning as you advance your business. You need to take advantage of all the training opportunities that come your way. This includes formal training classes, looking for and working with mentors, and learning from your peers. Learn everything you can from everyone around you, and realize that your learning will never stop. You can always get better at what you do. Success is a journey, not a destination.

2 Look like a commercial/investment agent and learn the language

To work effectively with commercial/investment clients as well as other agents, you must look and act like you know what you're doing, and you must understand the language that commercial investors and agents speak. Throughout the book, I teach you how to behave like a commercial/ investment agent and teach you the language you need to know. I also describe the formulas you'll most often use and how to apply them.

Fundamental to your success will be your ability to analyze properties correctly. In other words, you must learn how to determine what a property is at present and to assess what a property could be, and to do so by applying the correct factors and formulas regardless of what another agent might have done. In this book, I describe my four-step system for how to analyze a property the right way. Use it! It's indispensable to your success.

3 Run your business as a business

To have a successful commercial/investment real estate business, you must run your business as a business. Are you wondering why I even mention that? Does it seem obvious to you? Well, from my experience this is where many people go wrong.

Start by planning your time based on your goals and priorities and realize that as time goes on you can't allow yourself to be distracted from your goals and priorities.

Learn to focus on your priorities and delegate lower priority activities to others.

To be successful, you must also apply strategic systems that will be foundational to operating your business. I teach you how to develop and use four types of lead generating systems, of which the grid system is one. I emphasize that you must constantly work to generate new listings because listings are the heart of your business.

4 Focus on consulting

As I said earlier, consulting is all about helping clients understand the possibilities available to them. But the trick is to do it without talking down, and by engaging the client in the discussion.

To consult effectively, you must ask the right questions. Following are examples of what I mean: Why are you investing? Where do you see yourself in two years, in five years? In a perfect world, what is an ideal passive income goal for you? How long do you think it will take you to achieve this goal? If I can show you how to do this in X amount of time instead of Y amount of time, would that be valuable to you?

Of course, your clients will likely say something like, "Yes, that would be great, but can you do that?" When they do, respond by saying something like, "Well, yes, I can because I am a Certified Real Estate Investment Planning Specialist (CREIPS)™. I help people achieve their goals faster through written real estate planning strategies."

Do you see how these kinds of questions can open ideas for a client that they may not have considered before? In this book, I take this discussion to the next level with what I call elevator scripts. The scripts show you how to move through a planning and strategy discussion with a client by asking questions that will help you.

1) *educate the client*

2) *pinpoint the client's goals*

3) *identify the strategies the client wants to use to achieve those goals.*

5 Prepare written investment plans

You'll provide excellent value to your clients when you can help them define their goals and develop strategies for achieving those goals. But even then, you still have work to do. You need to give your clients a written real estate plan that describes the goals and how to achieve them. Before you invest your time, you must be sure that you and your client agree on what they want and on what you will do to help them achieve it.

*To receive the C.R.E.I.P.S. designation, completion of The NCREA's 3 Day Course is required.

Defining real estate investment goals, developing strategies, and writing real estate investment plans is a complex discussion. One reason is because investors can have widely differing goals, and investors can use different strategies to reach those goals. I plan a future book in which I develop these ideas in more detail, but from what you learn in this book, I hope that you'll realize these are important skills and that you'll begin using them in your business.

CHAPTER 2

HITTING YOUR TARGET

What do goal setting, time blocking, and delegating have in common? These activities point to critical differences between people who are successful and people who are not. Knowing how to set goals and plan your time accordingly are critical to your success.

1 Set Goals

People who set goals and stick to them are not flying by the seat of their pants, which is what many people tend to do. Most people simply react to what comes in. But if you are serious about meeting your goals, you will need to do things differently.

Start by defining your goals for the day, the week, and the month. You will need to work systematically.

2 Block your time

Next, time block, which means to assign blocks of time to the key activities that will help ensure you hit your goals for the day, the week, the month, and year. Do not do this only in your mind.

Use a calendar. It does not matter if you use paper, Google, or any other tool. Use the tool that works for you.

Plan your time Monday through Friday, or for whatever days you want to hold yourself accountable. If you still sell residential real estate, block out the time you plan to spend on that as well.

For commercial/investment activities, indicate each day the time you want to start and end, and what you want to achieve during each block of time. Then look at each week, month, and year, and identify your goals and plan your time accordingly.

For example, you might carve out two hours each day, maybe an hour in the morning and an hour later in the day. That would give you 10 hours a week to work toward your commercial/investment real estate goals.

During those blocks of time, do commercial/investment work only. Nothing else.

3 Focus on High-Dollar Activities

Are you wondering what you should focus on during the time you dedicate to your commercial/investment real estate goals? The answer is your high-dollar activities.

Here are what I refer to as high-dollar activities:

- *Prospecting*
- *Listing*
- *Selling*
- *Negotiating*

In the beginning, and as you build your business, your most critical job each day is looking for listings. I explain that in detail later.

To meet your goal of earning at least $100,000 next year in commercial/investment real estate, focus on these activities at all times.

Use the Three-Foot Rule

Okay, now that you have a schedule, you are going to stick to it no matter what. But we both know that can be hard to do.

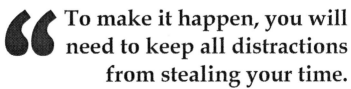

To make it happen, you will need to keep all distractions from stealing your time.

Statistics show that morning is the best time for getting things done. Plan to complete as much of your important work as you can during the morning hours. By the afternoon, life happens. Things come up and get in your way.

Avoid distractions by applying what I call the three-foot rule. When I am working, I do not allow anyone, or anything, into my three-foot circle.

Think of yourself as being in the center of a three-foot circle. Do not let anything into that circle other than commercial/investment activities. Do not allow anything — texts, phone calls, or someone knocking on the door — to interrupt your work. Remain committed to your success. No one and nothing can get in your way during the time you devote to commercial/investment work.

So, start the morning by turning off your phone, closing your door, and telling your family that you are busy and that you are not to be interrupted. Then, once you have achieved your time blocking goals for that day, you are free to do whatever needs your attention.

DELEGATING YOUR WAY TO SUCCESS

Over the years, I have had only a handful of assistants on my team. Having an assistant has meant that I have been able to take on more high-dollar work. It can work the same way for you.

The process of hiring an assistant can make anyone nervous. But it can also help elevate you to greater success. If you want to make more money, you need to fill your time with high-dollar work, not $8.00 an hour stuff. So even if the idea of hiring an assistant makes you nervous, focus on the benefits.

I did not understand the value of having an assistant until my first coach shared with me that he learned to delegate in order to achieve more and grow. Then I realized that to take on more volume, say if I wanted to add ten more listings a month, I would need to hire an assistant. True, I had to spend time looking for the right assistant. But once my new assistant and I were working well together, I did increase my listings. I managed to take on ten new listings a month. I hit my goal. Then I started moving things from my desk to hers, and soon my desk was empty. That left two options. Take some of that stuff back, or go out and take on more new business. I went for the new business and increased my profits.

Until I heard my coach's story, I had not considered how hiring an assistant could help improve my business. But it works. You can do the same. Put it out there, and then go get it!

Tips for Delegating

While you focus on your scheduled tasks, delegate everything else that needs to occur during that same time frame. Delegation is necessary to meeting your goals.

For example, your goal is to earn $100,000 selling commercial/investment over the next 12 months. To make this happen, realize that you will need to do things differently from what you have done in the past.

$100,000 in a 45-hour work week over 48 weeks means that you will need to make $45.00 an hour to make $100,000. So, what are your high-dollar activities? Anything that exceeds $45 an hour. For sure this does not include emailing, shooting the breeze, or playing on Facebook.

Your high-dollar activities are:

- *Prospecting*
- *Listing*
- *Selling*
- *Negotiating*

These are the four areas that you should focus on and make your priority. Get good at dedicating your time to high dollar activities, and delegating to low-dollar activities.

Here are some other ideas to consider. If you want to make $100,000 in half the time, work a couple of hours a week and delegate everything else. Or delegate everything you can and take five hours off every day, or take four months off during the year. My point is if you become efficient at delegating, you can reach your income goals faster and sooner than you might have thought.

1 Use a Virtual Assistant

You do not need to hire a full-time person. You can hire a virtual assistant to do the work you want to delegate. A virtual assistant is a person who may physically work in your office or not, who will work the hours you need them, and who may be a $3.00 to a $35 an hour person.

For assistants who are not in your office, you can work using email and the telephone, and you can use video conference tools like Skype.

You can also consider sharing a virtual assistant with two or three other people in your office. That allows you to share the cost, but be sure that you set clear and written time frames for when the person will work for you.

I try to hire people in the US because that has worked best for me, but that may not be the case in your situation. You can find virtual assistants on sites such as Upwork.com and numerous other sources on and offline.

2 Write a Job Description

A job description is a necessary thing, both for you and your assistant.

In preparation for hiring my first assistant, I wrote down the things I wanted the assistant to do. And I made sure it was a long list. I wanted to be sure my new assistant would have plenty to do. I also identified the key tasks I wanted to be done, and the strengths needed (people skills, technical skills such as using Word, and so on) to perform those tasks.

Most of us tend to hire people because we like them. If we like them, we hire them. But that is a terrible way to hire people. We like people typically because they are like us. But you probably need to hire someone with skills that are **opposite** of yours.

Another thing you might consider is the personality type of the assistant you hire. For example, you probably do not want to hire someone with a social personality for administrative work. You probably want someone who is good at using the computer and good with details, which is not typical of real estate agents.

Many personality assessments are available. Any of them can give you accurate, relevant, and important information about how different types of people approach their work. Do some research on the Internet to get some ideas and to help you think about the kind of person you might want to hire.

The key is to plan ahead for your assistant. Develop a job description by writing down the job standards, primary objectives, regular and most frequent work activities, managing responsibilities, key skills, and attitudes. If you need a sample description, check the Internet. But write all this information down. Who? Why? How often? Compensation, experience, education. Everything.

3 Conduct Screening Interviews

Once you have a complete job description, you are ready to interview candidates. Create a screening interview worksheet that you use in every interview. Include questions concerning work experience, education, life experience, and interests.

Then go over the job description with the person, assuming you did not do that earlier in the interview. Talk to the person about the job, what you are looking for in an assistant, and what your expectations are for how you can work together. Be real here. Do not act different than you do.

When you find the person you want to hire, have them sign the job description. That means they understand the job activities and they agree to do them. Having a signed job description can save problems later. Typically, when a problem arises, people say, "Oh, I didn't realize I was supposed to do that." You can say, "Well, wait a minute, here's where you agreed that you could do them. So, are you resigning?" Having a solid job description and a formal agreement from the person to perform those duties will help you when you need to hold the person accountable.

I have done a bit of hiring over the years and can provide more specific help to you on this topic. If you need assistance, let me know. I am happy to be a resource for you.

4 Set Mutual Expectations

You will also need to set mutual expectations with the person you plan to hire. It is a separate and important step. Discuss questions such as how do you win with me? How do I win with you? How do you lose with me? How do I lose with you? How do you want me to handle sensitive situations with you? This is how I want you to handle sensitive situations with me, and so on.

Discuss all the scenarios that might arise, and then write down and sign the agreed-to expectations, just as you did with the job duties. The point is you want to avoid possible misunderstandings. If you do this, chances are you will have a good relationship with this person. And then it is all about training and leading them. It is also critical that you make them feel like a vital part of your business. A valued employee is a loyal employee.

For tools and resources to help you with this, visit my blog at www.TheNCREA.com, and type in mutual expectations.

CHAPTER 4

TAKING ADVANTAGE ON THE CURRENT MARKET

I n my opinion, several trends are currently in play, and these trends are working to expand the opportunities for participating in commercial/investment real estate.

In fact, these trends are creating more opportunities than ever before. And now is the time for you to take advantage of them.

Residential Companies Establishing Commercial/ Investment Divisions

Many of the large residential real estate companies already have, or they are in the process of developing, commercial/ investment real estate divisions. Do you wonder why they are doing this?

The answer is money, right?

Most of these firms have large research and development divisions, and they are typically busy researching trends to identify the best opportunities for their firms. And it is obvious commercial/investment real estate is one big trend. These companies are seeking opportunities for participating in commercial/investment transactions and making profits, and at the same time helping more people achieve their goals.

You must ask yourself if they are researching and developing their commercial/investment real estate activity, why shouldn't I do so as well?

Adding commercial/investment to your skills will likely make a difference in your earnings, and it will also be a valuable experience for you. No matter where you work, adding commercial/investment real estate to your portfolio can only help your career.

Let me be clear. I am not suggesting that a real estate agent or investor should step outside their area of expertise and work in areas they do not understand.

What I am suggesting is that you get the training you need and that you consider adding commercial/investment services to your portfolio. You will be able to help more people and to earn more money at the same time. But to do that, you must be a commercial/investment real estate professional. You must know what you are doing. Proper training and education are essential to your success.

Cap Rates and the Current Business Environment

I have another reason for believing it is a great time to add commercial/investment to your portfolio. It is why I say there may never be another opportunity better than now.

In most areas, Cap Rates are going down. In the commercial/investment environment, we call that cap rate compression. Cap rates compressing means that prices are going up.

But there is another important factor to understand. Currently, we have a window of opportunity that will likely close, and likely will never be as large as it is now. As Cap Rates continue to trend downward, interest rates are trending upward. And they will likely continue trending upward. They cannot get much lower for much longer than they are right now.

In most areas, interest rates are lower than Cap Rates for the first time in commercial/investment real estate history.

As interest rates continue to trend upward, and Cap Rates continue to trend downward, there will come a point when this window of opportunity will go away, and the window will close for quite some time. Most of us will never see this again in our lifetimes.

The ability to purchase during this window is a "perfect storm" of commercial/investment opportunities, like the residential opportunities that in most areas have already come and gone. So, it is important that you act now.

Realtor Associations Promoting Commercial/ Investment Activities

The other trend I want to mention is that real estate organizations such as the California Association of Realtors, the Chicago Association of Realtors, and the National Association of Realtors are launching, or attempting to launch, committees, forums, and other groups to assist residential agents in commercial/investment transactions. You can get support from these groups as you move into the commercial/ investment industry.

Again, ask yourself, why are realtor associations developing commercial/investment resources?

Again, the answer is money. These organizations recognize the opportunity to receive revenue and grow membership by helping you facilitate commercial/ investment transactions.

If these entities understand the big opportunity in commercial/investment real estate, why shouldn't you also understand and seize the moment?

Another reason, in my opinion, is that never have we seen more cooperation and more desire to help the residential real estate agent and investor learn how to be successful in commercial/ investment real estate transactions. I have sometimes heard people say, "Oh, you cannot do both. You cannot be successful in both residential and commercial (Resimercial). It is not possible."

I think I have proven this is not the case. It is possible to do both. All the trends I described here validate is it possible to do both. If you desire to do both, you should consider doing so.

Why do I say that?

Residential and Commercial are Compatible

As a residential agent, you already have relationships with clients, friends, and acquaintances. These relationships will go a long way toward helping you achieve success in the commercial/investment world.

The average person wants to work with someone they know and trust. They do not want to build a relationship with someone new. What holds them back, the issue that bothers them, is they are not sure you are capable of facilitating their commercial/investment transactions.

What you must do is show up and ask for the order. But before you do that, be sure you are qualified, trained in the area the person is interested in, and that you know how to get the job done.

No one can interfere with the relationships you have already developed. Full-time commercial real estate agents are starting to understand that the relationships between residential agents and their clients cannot be penetrated.

CHAPTER 5

SHARPENING YOUR SAW

It is vital that you recognize the importance of education in meeting your commercial/investment real estate goals. The commercial/investment industry is constantly transforming, and the laws and regulations are constantly changing as well. And now with social media so widely in play, the industry is more dynamic than ever.

The real estate industry is complicated, and the commercial/investment real estate industry can be particularly complex. To be successful, you will need to learn and improve consistently. It is critical that you understand you will need to continue learning as long as you are in the industry, and that any shortcuts could be costly.

" You must commit to continuing training and professional education if you expect to achieve the success you desire.

I am amused when someone tells me they do not have time to attend a training event, or they say, "Oh, I already know all that." Inevitably, when this person does attend an event, I see that they do not know "all that." They do need professional training.

An easy way to find out if you have mastered something is to teach it. Nothing compares to being in front of 30 or more people and having questions thrown at you.

When you can comfortably teach a subject, then it may be okay to say that you have a good understanding of the content. Then you are ready to continue your education. There will always be new things to learn, especially in the commercial/ investment industry.

I grew up in Oregon, and I like to share the story of two woodcutters at a woodcutting contest. Both had a coach.

The first contestant was busy cutting down his tree, and at one point his coach advised him to stop and sharpen his saw. The contestant said, "No, no I don't want to lose ground. I don't have time to stop and sharpen my saw."

The second contestant also had a coach, and this coach said the same thing, to stop and sharpen the saw. The second contestant listened to his coach and stopped to sharpen his saw several times. Who do you think won the race?

That's correct. The contestant who took the time to stop and sharpen his saw cut down the most trees in the time allowed.

This is an important story to remember in a world with a microwave mentality (give it to me, and give it all to me now!)

Did you know?

To be successful in real estate, 3% - 5% of your income should be dedicated to training. The industry changes rapidly. You should always be learning.

CHAPTER 6

SEPARATING YOURSELF FROM YOUR COMPETITION

O ne of my skills is the ability to separate myself from everyone else. I know how to stand apart. I know how to jump out from the competition, and I am not afraid to be unique.

It is important to follow the models put forth by successful people. Yes, that is certainly something I have learned to do. However, after you establish your commercial/investment business on a stable, successful foundation, you can then be creative and build on that foundation.

But the opposite is not true. If you try to be creative as the foundation of your business, you will have an unstable business model. If you build your business without following a successful model, you will significantly decrease your chance of success. Remember my earlier failure story?

1 **Be Unique:** Consider having an USP (Unique Selling Proposition)

Assuming you have professional education in the commercial/investment industry, and assuming you have the confidence to work a deal, you are now in a position where you need to start being creative. Now you need to figure out what you have that will make you stand out from the crowd. With all the other real estate agents out there in your area, what can you do to stand out, to look different and be unique, so that you do not blend in with all the other agents?

If I were to ask you to send me samples of your marketing—your business cards, website templates, email templates, marketing flyers, and so on—would yours look different from what everyone else uses? Or would yours blend in?

In upcoming chapters, I will share some ways that you can separate yourself from the competition so that you stand out and are unique.

2 **Look Commercial**

You may not have thought about developing your commercial/investment image, the image you present to your investor clients, but if you want to be successful in the industry, you will need to look the part.

Hey, I have nothing against looking residential. You may be doing fine in the residential world and be satisfied with your look. That is great. But what I am telling you is that look may not work in the commercial/investment world.

> **66 The residential and commercial/investment worlds are not the same. Commercial/ investment investors will shy away from you if you look residential.**

Google yourself. How do you look? Do you look like a realtor an investor would trust? If not, think about making some changes.

What I am talking about here is not your specific physical characteristics, and not necessarily your wardrobe or car. I am talking about that quality of self-assurance that tells your prospects that you know what you are doing and that you can get their job done.

First, believe in yourself. Assuming you have been taking classes and working to develop your expertise in commercial/investment real estate, you deserve to look the part.

Start by changing things around. The purpose is to convince yourself that you are taking on a new endeavor and that you need a new demeanor to go along with it. Be confident that you have the knowledge to advise people on their real estate investment goals.

Look at your email and business cards; take a fresh look at all your marketing material. This review will take some time, and has some costs involved, but it is important that you show up with confidence at a meeting with a commercial/investment prospect.

Understand that the investors you will talk with are real people, normal people, and you will need to know what to communicate to them, and how to communicate it. Start now.

Success Tip:

At TheNCREA.com/Blog you will find a checklist to help you with this. Enter How to Look Commercial in the Search field.

CHAPTER 7

LEARNING TO SPEAK THE LANGUAGE

Would you agree that if a prospect or a buyer walked into your open house, or they called you or ran into you somewhere, the investor would soon understand whether you knew what you were talking about?

Yes, as you soon as you started speaking, the investor would know whether you had the knowledge to handle their potential transaction.

The commercial/investment industry has a language of its own, and as with any other language, you will need to learn to speak it.

Upside potential. Do you know what that means? "I'm looking for something with upside potential," is probably the most common statement I hear from investors.

What if a potential buyer asked you if a property was a value play? Would you know what that commercial/ investment buyer was asking?

In the How to List & Sell Commercial Investment Property Companion Guide, I go over terms that are essential to the industry like:

- upside potential
- value add
- vanilla
- value play
- horizontal vs. vertical investing

Success Tip:

If you still need help with this after going through the Companion Guide, check out one of our 1 Day Live Trainings or Online Courses.

CHAPTER 8

CONSULTING VERSUS SELLING

I previously pointed out the importance of being unique, of standing out from the competition and separating yourself from everyone else. One of the ways you can do that is by using commercial/investment language. But, there are other ways as well.

Have you attended a commercial/investment networking event? If so, you probably know that when you network with investors, you often have 30 to 60 seconds to introduce yourself and to find out a little bit about the other person.

During this short window of time, your main objective is to make a connection, with the idea that you can follow up with the person later.

Your goal is to be different, to stand out so that the person wants to talk with you again, and even to work with you versus anyone else.

You have a minute or less to build rapport with the person, and at the same time let them know that you are the right person for the job.

Early in my career, at this point, I would sell. What I mean is, I would talk about myself, about how great I am. For example, I would say:

• "I am in the top one percent of all agents in the United States" or

• "I am the number three commercial/investment agent in the states of California and Hawaii" or

• "I sell a property every four and a half days"

• "I sold over 100 properties alone" and so on.

What I learned is the average person does *not* care about me or my track record, or how many properties I have sold, or that I am number one.

Who does the average investor care about first and foremost, above and beyond anything else?

Yes, that is correct. The average investor, the average person, for that matter, cares about themselves. What does this mean to me? The average person listens to the station WIIFM -- What's In It For Me?

> **If you know how to consult, as opposed to trying to sell yourself, you will be much more effective in establishing rapport and building a relationship.**

You see, when you consult you are asking questions. You are drawing the person toward you. When you are selling, you are bragging, talking about yourself. Selling is like throwing up all over the person, and nine times out of ten they will run from it. Whereas when you consult, you ask about the person's interests and concerns, and that draws them to you.

Consulting is also effective because sometimes the other person does not think they need to learn anything new. Thinking we already know everything about a subject is a common mindset.

But by asking the right questions, carefully thought out questions you have planned in advance, you can make the person curious to know more, or to think maybe I should talk with this commercial/investment realtor and find out what he knows.

I call these pre-planned questions *elevator scripts*. They are the questions you ask almost every time you meet someone new.

Here's How it Works:

Imagine yourself walking into a room and meeting a client or potential investor. But wait a minute. Do you agree that almost anyone you meet is a potential investor? You should.

So, imagine yourself talking to anyone about commercial/ investment real estate.

You might think that you should start by telling the person all about your listings. But no, that is not where you need to be.

> **When you start talking with someone, what you need to be thinking about is what might be stopping this person from deciding to invest.**

Money and fear are what typically hold people back from investing in commercial/investment real estate. The fear could come from a lack of experience or a lack of knowledge. A fearful prospect will have trouble making the decision to buy.

Establish Rapport

So where do you begin? What do you talk about first? It seems obvious, but I do not want to assume anything, so let me digress for a moment. When you first meet someone, start by establishing a rapport with them. An easy way to do that is to spend a few minutes asking about the person's family, occupation, what they like to do for recreation, and most important of all, their dreams. I remember this with FORD:

F	**Family**
O	**Occupation**
R	**Recreation**
D	**Dreams**

For more info on elevator scripts and how they work, see the Companion Guide, available through Amazon.com and TheNCREA.com.

DISCOVERING DREAMS AND WRITING A PLAN

Remember, when establishing rapport, ask the person about their family, occupation, recreation, and dreams (remember by thinking FORD). For example, you might ask about the person's children or what they like to do for fun. Or you could ask about their dreams by asking where the person sees themselves in two years or five years. I also suggest you ask why the person wants to invest in real estate.

I use these questions to get an investor thinking about WHY they are doing something. If you can help people tap into their deep "Why," and help them articulate it, you can help them create a written real estate investment plan, which will go a long way toward helping them achieve their goal with your personal goals and strategies, you need to write down your investor's plan. It is not enough to have your investor's plan in your mind or their mind. You both need to review and agree to a plan on paper.

So, spend a significant amount of time on dreams.

Most people are investing in real estate in hopes of future earnings. Sure, they might have cash flow today or want cash flow today. I think when someone says, "I'm looking for something with cash flow," that means they do not want a negative cash flow. They do not want an animal they must feed.

Most investors I have met do not demand a lot of cash flow from the particular property to live off, to pay bills, or to support themselves. In my experience, most investors are investing because they want to create a certain amount of passive income in the future.

For example, an investor may have "dreams" (a goal) of having a $100,000 of passive income in 10 years. They dream of retiring and living on their passive income stream. Part of your value is helping investors discover at a high level what it is they want, which is why they are investing.
You can help them articulate their goals and dreams, and you can give it to them in writing, in the form of a written real estate investment plan. No doubt you need to know your numbers, the Return on Investment, and all the formulas. But I will share with you that most of your success will come from applying that information to reality and helping investors achieve their goals FASTER. I can tell you that because my success has come in this way.

For example, if you know that an investor's goal is $100,000 passive income in 10 years, you can ask more questions. First, ask questions to learn the details of that goal. Then ask the investor if you could show them how to achieve that goal of $100,000 in half the time, say five years or seven years, and would that be of interest to them?

What are they going to say?

Of course, they are interested in learning the strategies you can help them use to achieve their goal in less time. Then it becomes a matter of trust. Does the person trust you? If so, you can move into the details of the strategies you are recommending.

Do you see how it is so important to help someone; how important it is to find out the person's goals and dreams?

How many people have specific goals?

Now, how many people do you think have their goals in writing? Of those who have their goals in writing, how many people look at them every day? My guess is you are probably thinking of smaller and smaller percentages as you go along, and I agree with that.

Now ask yourself how many of those people have someone who holds them accountable for reaching their goals. By the way, a major key to success, and typically the difference between those who achieve their goals and those who do not, is having someone who holds them accountable for reaching their goals.

So remember, it is a simple as 1, 2, 3:

1) *Help investors set goals.*

2) *Help investors write their goals and strategies in an investment plan.*

3) *Advise investors to find someone who will hold them accountable for reaching their goals.*

The reason I am talking about this is so you will think about the large number of people who are investing in real estate without a written real estate investment plan. They may not even have specific criteria or goals in writing.

When you understand this, you will understand why they need your assistance. You can put your professional education and experience to good use. The demand is high. If you can help an investor create a written real estate investment plan, you will provide a great service, and you will make more money in the long run.

With a written real estate investment plan, your investor will be clear on what they want and they will be committed to achieving it, and you are just the person to help them do it.

CHAPTER 10

TALKING TO A LISTING BROKER

Maybe you just received a call from a client whose home you sold years ago. And you, being the great agent that you are, have kept in touch with this client. And we know all agents do a great job of keeping in touch with past clients. Right? Yeah, right.

The client tells you they saw a property for sale down the street from their house. All they saw was a for sale sign on a commercial/investment building. They ask if you will help them get some information about the property.

What will you say? I would guess your answer is probably something like sure, I can help you with that.

What would you do next, when you were still on the phone with this person? If your answer is you should set an appointment, you are correct.

Research the Property

What should you find out about the property before you meet with your client?

Here are a few things I suggest. Drive by the property. I do not suggest walking on the property, and certainly, you should not disturb any tenants, but driving by is always good.

Determine whether the property has deferred maintenance and assess its general condition. Check for parking, laundry, whether the property has a pool, elevators, and courtyards. You should also determine if it is a Class A, B, or C property type.

Also, assess the area. Rate the neighborhood as poor, fair, good, or excellent. Does the neighborhood have similar property types, or is this property different from everything else in the area? Is the property near powerlines, an airport or runways, or maybe a freeway? You would do more due diligence at this point, similar to what you would do for residential regarding location.

Consider checking LoopNet.com. It is a major source for commercial/investment real estate properties that are for sale. You might also review the Multiple Listing Service (MLS) to determine if this property has ever been listed, or possibly is listed for sale now.

Consider Googling the address. You may also want to review the title and property profile to get the basics of owner name, property size, square footage, year built, and so on.

So, let's say you have completed your due diligence, and let's assume you could not find much if any information about the property online. However, you did see a sign on the property. Now you need to call the listing broker to get more information. Do you know what to ask for when you call or email a commercial/investment broker?

Ask for the Set Up or Marketing Package

Set Up package and Marketing package are common terms you will hear. Sometimes these packages are also called Offering Memorandums (OM), although that is rare. The Set Up or Marketing package contains information about a commercial/investment property that is for sale.

So one of the first things you want to do is contact the listing broker and ask for the Set Up. You might say, "I'm interested in such and such a property. Can you send me the Set Up?"

Students tell me they are sometimes anxious when they call the commercial/investment broker because maybe the broker will know they do not work full-time in commercial/ investment real estate and that they do some residential. Sometimes people think the commercial/investment agent will not want to cooperate. Have you experienced that problem?

Well, I do not think the situation is that the commercial/investment agent does not want to cooperate. Think about it like this. How many agents do you know who like to work with agents on the other end of the deal who have no idea about what they are doing?

How do you like working with such an agent?

I am going to take a wild guess and say that you do not like to work with an agent who does not know what they are doing. Most of us do not. Nobody wants to feel like they are doing all the work and still must share the compensation.

If you contact the commercial/investment listing broker, and you sound like a residential agent or an agent who does not know what they are doing, well then, sure, the listing agent will probably hesitate to send information or work with you.

For example, if you ask questions like "I'm wondering if the property is still available, can I show it tomorrow, or does the property have a lock box," the commercial/investment broker will think "no way do I want to get involved in a transaction with this agent."

On the other hand, if you sound confident and professional, like someone who can get the job done, the chances are the commercial/investment broker is going to work with you because they want to get their listing sold and get paid, just like everyone else.

To view a powerfully effective script for talking with listing brokers, see the Companion Guide.

Success Tip:

You can also find trainings with demonstrations on how to use scripts at TheNCREA.com.

CHAPTER 11

LEAD GENERATION

I often ask business owners, "What business are you in?" Inevitably I get all kinds of answers. Some say, "The real estate business!" Others say, "The commercial/investment business!" Some even say, "The closing business!"

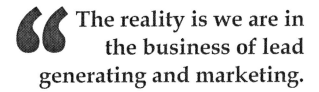 **The reality is we are in the business of lead generating and marketing.**

It does not matter how much we know, how smart we are, or how experienced we are if we do not have any leads. Do you agree? One of the keys to being successful, and hands down the most important, is lead generation. To have success, you must have leads, and the "s" at the end means more than one lead!

Wake up every work day and ask yourself this: How many new leads can I get today?

Your goal is to have six to eight conversations every single day. That is how you fill your pipeline with new leads.

Yes, I mean it. Every day you must have six to eight conversations with new people who might be interested in buying or selling commercial/investment properties.

Yes, the constant search for leads is difficult and time- consuming. But things will be even more difficult if you do not contact six to eight leads every day. In a short time, you will be stuck and maybe close to being out of work. Or maybe you will try to play catch up by calling more people some days. That does not work either.

Think about it. If I said I would pay you $100 to have six to eight conversations tomorrow (and for every day you did), you would find a way to do it, and you would show up looking for your hundred bucks!

Make a Plan and Stick to the Plan

Are you starting to understand that achieving your leads goal is a matter of focus, a matter of priority and time blocking your daily activities? Time blocking is the simple difference between the top producer and everyone else. Successful agents plan their day, every day, in advance, and they do not deviate from their plan.

Another way to improve your lead generation process is to establish systems that will drive leads your way. That will make it much easier to have those six to eight new conversations every day.

What is a Lead Generating System?

A lead generation system is a way of generating leads with little daily effort. Working with a system means working smart. You will Save Your Self Time, Energy, and Money when you work a system!

Putting systems in place does take effort in the beginning, but you will soon pick up momentum and see the advantages. Understand that this is a long-term plan. In most cases, you will not see immediate results, but you will realize long-term results.

Ideally, you should have four lead generating systems in place. These four systems will help funnel those daily six to eight conversations to you.

As time goes on and your business grows, these systems can and most likely will change, but for now, here are the most productive systems you can develop (based on your skills and personality):

- *Referral sphere (people you already know)*
- *Grid (sellers, listings both on and off the market, or "pocket" listings)*
- *Internet (buyers)*
- *Market of the moment (respond to market conditions)*

When you get good at using these systems, the sky is the absolute limit.

Think about matching your personality and skills to the first system you put in place. For example, some agents are more social, whereas other agents are especially good with numbers. What I mean is, do you like to work with sellers? Do you like to work with buyers? Do you prefer telephone or email, or do you prefer face-to-face networking and knocking on doors?

If you do not know where to start, do what I suggest below and start with your Referral Sphere system. But if you have a preference, for example, if you like to work with buyers, consider starting with your Internet system.

Following is an overview of the four lead generating systems. In the next few chapters, I describe each system in more detail.

Referral Sphere System

The Grid system is my number one recommended system. However, your Referral Sphere system is made up of people who know you, so it is a good starting point. Unlike the Grid, which is cold, your Referral Sphere system is an easier place to start.

Grid System (Sellers)

After you have your Referral Sphere system working, implement your Grid system. It will mostly generate sellers. The Grid system is the most important system. It is pure gold. I can't recommend it highly enough.

Internet System

The third system to implement is the Internet system. It will mostly generate buyers, so we also call it a buyer system.

Market-of-the-Moment System

The fourth system is the market-of-the-moment. It is a dynamic system, a system that changes depending on current trends. You act by responding to market conditions. Examples could be marketing REOs, Expireds, Short Sales,etc. depending on your present market.

Build One System at a Time

How many systems do you think you should put together when you first start? If you answered one, you are correct. How many systems do you think the average agent tries to implement when starting? If you answered all four, you are correct!

The average person tries to do everything at once and typically ends up being overwhelmed. Start with your first system. Get it up and spinning (working effectively). Then add a second system, then a third, and then a fourth.

For more info on building your lead generation systems, see the Companion Guide, or visit TheNCREA.com.

CHAPTER 12

HOW TO SECURE COMMERCIAL BUYERS

I decided to discuss investment buyers in this book because this seems to be the area where I get the most questions. "Michael, I have a buyer. What do I do? What do I say? How can I find a property for them?"

My passion and strength have always been in working with sellers. I have been a listing agent my entire career, both in residential and commercial/investment real estate. The seller side is more complicated and has more sources for getting seller listings, but I receive more questions about buyers. So, I decided to discuss buyers here, just as I do in my one-day training events.

This section discusses the two main ways to secure buyers and then ways to work with your buyers.

But first, a word of caution. Buyers are everywhere, and they are a distraction from sellers. All investors are buyers. Look at your time and think about how you are distributing your time among sellers, networking, and buyers. Start breaking down your calendar.

If you are having success with your calendar, in other words, you are on track to get the number of listings you want, then you may be ready to work with more buyers. But if you are not having success yet, that is, you are not on track (you are struggling and cannot find the time to get the number of listings you want), then you should not bring in buyers. We are listing agents. We should be going after listings. We have a certain number of hours to work with to get listings, and that needs to be the priority.

The bottom line is you cannot spend all your time with buyers, and you need to keep that in mind as you plan your schedule.

Prospecting for Buyers

You can secure buyers in two ways. I call the first the fall- on-your-plate-buyers. The second way is that you prospect for buyers.

It is easy to handle the fall-on-your-plate buyers. What is your number one goal? Right, to get an appointment with that buyer! They will want you to tell them what you have on the phone. But you are not going to discuss your properties on the phone because you know it is vital to have an in- person meeting.

You must use caution and be strict about your process. Buyers will push. They will say, "Can't you just send me something?" Beware of falling into that trap. It will cost you time and money. Your conversion rate will be higher when you meet in person.

You have four ways, or systems, which you can use to prospect for buyers. We have discussed them, but they are critical to your success, so I will review them here.

Grid System

This works for buyers as well as sellers. Your Grid system will generate buyers for you because everybody is a buyer. When you contact your Grid, you will be looking for sellers. But clients are always going to inquire about properties to purchase. They will want to know if you have any good deals. Trust me; you will find buyers within your Grid system.

Internet System

Another name for the Internet System is the Buyers System, and technology provides you with several ways to go about using it.

You must have a website. A website is your main vehicle. The number one thing people are looking for is properties. Your website should be all about properties for sale, maybe some properties you have sold and other helpful information specific to the area such as statistics (i.e. cap rates, lease rates, etc.)

But the real purpose of your site is, what it should be about, is lead conversion. And in case you are wondering, your website should not be about "stuff" (agents, recipes, and resumes).

1031 Exchanges

The third way to prospect for buyers is through 1031 exchanges. Go to your title company and ask if they can give you a list of everybody who is going through a 1031 exchange right now.

They may be hesitant to give the information due to confidentiality, but if you dig, dig and dig, you will find a source who will give that information.

Sometimes the exchange clients are awesome. Perhaps a client is going through a delayed exchange, which means they are under certain time requirements to close escrow, or they may have tax consequences. If you are in that position and you do not purchase something you will pay the IRS. Or, do you go ahead and close and pay a little more than market value and avoid paying the IRS? You are probably willing to pay a little over market value to avoid paying the IRS.

Tenants and Business Owners

The fourth prospecting source is contacting business owners or people who are renting or leasing commercial/investment properties. This is a great way to find buyers.

CHAPTER 13

DON'T BE A JACK-OF-ALL-TRADES AND MASTER OF NONE

I advise everyone starting out in commercial/investment real estate to pick an area and to become an expert in that specific area.

I also urge you to master one product type, or at the most, two product types. Find something you like or have strength in, and or a niche that you have started already, and get good at it. Master it. Do not try to do too many different things or too many product types.

Maybe you know a client who is in the hospitality industry, and you have done a bed-and-breakfast for them. This is an example of what I mean when I say perhaps you have already started something. In my opinion, you are better off building on that and getting good at it, mastering the hospitality product types, and sticking to them.

Most of the commercial/investment real estate brokers I have met concentrate on one specific product type, and they do it for a long time, meaning 30, 40, or 50 years.

I started with multifamily apartments and have also done some land, office, retail, industrial, and churches, a little bit of everything because I have received referrals. But I have done a lot of apartments in multifamily, and I got good at it. I can do them faster and easier, and frankly, I do a better job with that product type.

Every time I venture off into another product type that I have never done it is like I am working with my weaknesses instead of focusing on my strengths.

The same goes for you. You are better off succeeding at a high level by focusing on your strengths, mastering one or two product types, and getting good at that.

Recommendations for New Agents

If you are a new commercial/investment agent, and you have not decided on a property type, I recommend that you begin by specializing in multifamily.

Why do I recommend multifamily? It is not just because I specialize in them. One of the main reasons is that multifamily apartments are the easiest of all the product types to understand.

We have all lived in an apartment at one time, or at least we all know someone who did. Also, the owners of multifamily apartments are typically less sophisticated and easier to communicate with than many other kinds of investors. And they are usually dealing with month-to-month tenants who are also not super sophisticated. Finally, locating and meeting this type of investor is not complicated.

If you look at some of the other product types, for example, retail, those property owners are typically dealing with other business owners and communicating about complicated leases and negotiations. So, these investors tend to be more sophisticated. That does not mean that you cannot list and sell those product types. But it does mean that you are usually going to need a bit more experience to be as successful. Another factor to consider is financing. When you look at all the different product types available in commercial/investment real estate, multifamily apartments are typically one of the easier products to obtain financing on from the lender perspective.

One of the things lenders look at is risk, and multifamily apartments are one of the least risky investments.

Another reason I like multifamily apartments is that when real estate markets shift, multifamily apartments tend to stay somewhat stable as compared to other product types. Think about when a recession hits. Office space stops getting leased, consumers stop buying retail products, which affects the retail industry, and manufacturers stop manufacturing as much product. However, people still need a place to live. In some cases, properties even increase in value. People lose their homes, and they need a place to rent, so the demand for rentals may continue.

This does not mean that you must do multifamily. But if you have not already started working with one particular property type, multifamily is a good choice, at least until you have more experience.

Challenges in Working with More than One Property Type

If you should become involved in more than one or two product types, be aware of another challenge you will face. You will need to obtain the various tools and services that are required to close the transactions.

For example, if I am looking for a church, I may be able to find what I am looking for on LoopNet. If I am looking for an industrial building, I may not see it on LoopNet. I may only possibly see it through a service called Smith guide. This is just one example of what I mean when I say the tools and services that we need can be specific to product types. So, you are better off not trying to be a jack of all trades and a master of none. Agreed?

Okay, if you want an exception, the only one I can think of is if you are in a rural area where you do not have many products available or various types of sales you can do. In that situation, you have no choice but to do a little bit of everything.

CHAPTER 14

COMMERCIAL REAL ESTATE TOOLS

If you are a residential agent who is interested in commercial/investment real estate, I encourage you to start learning now. There is money to be made in commercial/ investment real estate, especially in the current market. What holds you back is not having the professional education you need and not believing you can be successful in commercial/investment real estate.

Start by going after some of the less expensive commercial/investment properties. You have great contacts and relationships in your residential database. Use them!

Take classes and continue learning about the commercial/investment industry and the tools available in your geographical area. Pick a specialty, and learn all you can about it, and learn about the tools that apply to that specialty. Become an expert, and let the people in your world know you can help them with their commercial/investment goals.

The National Commercial Real Estate Association (The NCREA)

The National Commercial Real Estate Association (The NCREA) offers various training and consulting programs to agents, real estate brokers, and investors. We offer two hour, one day, and three-day events, and monthly and annual programs. Our one-day event is approved for seven hours of continuing education under CalBre no. 5129. Our three-day event is approved for 21 hours of continuing education under CalBre no. 5129.

Contact The NCREA to find out more about the various programs offered and to schedule a training event near you. *www.facebook.com/TheNationalCommercialRealEstateAssociation www.TheNCREA.com Info@TheNCREA.com 877-877-1543. You can also join our Facebook group community at Facebook.com/ groups/TheNationalCommercialRealEstateAssociation where you can network with other professionals, ask questions and more.*

My YouTube Videos

I give demonstrations of my elevator scripts on YouTube. *www.youtube.com/c/michaelsimpsonthencrea*

Customer Relationship Management (CRM) Software

If you wonder which system to use, contact me through our Facebook Group @TheNationalCommercialAssociation. We have a lot of experience with these systems and can help you pick one that suits your needs.

Commercial/Investment Listings

Many commercial/investment listings are off market or pocket listings, but you can check these sites for those that are on the market:

- LoopNet is a database of commercial/investment listings. *www.loopnet.com*
- CoStar provides a variety of information of interest to commercial/investment professionals. www.costar.com

LoopNet and CoStar are the primary national sites. Depending on your city and state, you can likely find other sites as well.

Professional Organizations

Networking with national commercial/investment real estate associations and your local commercial/investment associations will provide you with many benefits. These organizations are actively supporting commercial/investment realtors, and networking with these groups is a great way to find pocket listings.

For example, Realty Investment Association of California (RIAOC) is a great place to find information on networking groups.

Google for information and check with other agents in your community. Ask, and you will begin to realize they are all around you.

CHAPTER 15

HOW TO FIND NEW BUSINESS

W hat should you do during the time you have blocked out for commercial/investment activities? Recall, at the beginning of this book, I advised that you focus on the high- dollar activities of prospecting, listing, negotiating, and selling. Those activities are where you need to focus your efforts.

But there is more that you can do. Unlike the residential world, commercial/investment transactions often start by word of mouth. Pocket listings are common, and the only way you will know about them is by getting out and talking to people.

You will learn all kinds of interesting things about what is happening in the commercial/investment world, and in your area, by taking the time to talk to other professionals.

Investment Clubs

Investment clubs are a great place to find out about off- market or pocket listings; to equip yourself with the commercial/investment lingo; and to meet people in the commercial/investment world. Do some research, and you will find some investment clubs in your area.

A good place to start is your local real estate board association. If you have several in your area, check with all of them for commercial/investment meetings, training, and events. When blocking your time, be aware that investment clubs typically meet once a week.

Networking Events and Investing Meetup Groups

In addition, apartment associations in your area may hold training events or networking events. You want to attend any of these you can find.

Investing meetup groups (Investing.Meetup.com) are another effective way to network. Your mission is to find where these events take place and to attend as many as possible. Beginning is a little difficult because these groups can be cliquish, but over time, you will be able to penetrate those barriers. Learn how the groups function and jump in.

Another option is for you to become an investment expert in your area. For example, you could host a training seminar every month. You might bring in a CPA or an attorney, and you give a talk on real estate. In effect, this becomes a marketing event for you. You just need to find the space, fill the room by advertising the event, and bring some wine and cheese or other snacks. Do not stop if your first event is not well attended. It may take time for your events to pick up steam. Have a plan and commit to it. Have a team to help you, and over time you will build steam.

The Grid System

The Grid system is one of the four lead-generating systems you need to use. To assist you, you can watch my YouTube videos on how to target investors strategically.

I also suggest that you go to LoopNet.com. Search for buildings in your area that meet you desired grid criteria. The Grid System is also a great way to get pocket listings. I have had a ton of success with this. Create a watch list on LoopNet and start educating yourself on these products.

Referrals

The number one source of business for commercial/investment associates is referrals. These include referrals from your office and your sphere of peers.

If you are in a residential office, be aware that agents in your office are sending commercial/investment work outside of your office right now! That is because they likely do not know anyone who handles commercial/investment transactions.

Announce yourself! Make them aware that you have the training and professional expertise to handle commercial/ investment transactions. When your colleagues realize that you have valid credentials, they will send those referrals to you.

If your Grid system is cold, start with your peers and your sphere of influence. Show up and be the commercial/ investment person they can trust to get the job done.

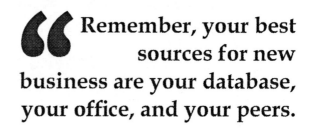 Remember, your best sources for new business are your database, your office, and your peers.

Newsletter

Here are other ideas. Start a newsletter and use it to keep in contact with people, and to introduce yourself to new people. Tell them things they want to know. Take your area of expertise and expound on it. Give people information about what is happening now, and tell them how they can take advantage of the information. For example, if you know all about apartments in the area, tell people what is happening in the apartment market, and let them know in what area they can find a deal (communicate what apartments are selling for, the cap rates, statistics, and so on).

Put out a glossy newsletter in color. You can burn copies of the outside (to save money) and customize the inside with new material.

Then make black and white copies, which helps with the cost, and mail them to everyone in your office and all the residential agents in your city. Most of these agents already know you as a good residential agent. When they learn that you are also in commercial, they will start sending their referrals to you.

CHAPTER 16

DEVELOPING YOUR MASTER PLAN

Where do you want to be in two years? Where do you want to be in five years? Where do you want to be in ten years?

Think about it. Do you realize that five years will go by even if you do not have a plan?

Without a plan, what will you have achieved?

What are your strategies for this year, for next year, and the next few years?

How do you start realizing your goals?

Write Down What You Want to Achieve

Start by writing down what you want to achieve. If you find yourself unable to define your desires, look into the future and pretend that it is five years from now. How do you picture that future? What are you doing? How much money are you making?

Now, work backward. What do you need to do to make that dream a reality? Make a complete list of all the things you want to achieve, and then order your items by what you need to do first, what you need to do second, and so on.

Once you have your goals identified, analyze the strategies you will need to follow to turn your goals into reality.

This really works. Trust me. It has worked for me as well as for hundreds of other people I have consulted, coached, and trained.

Write Your Master Plan

Map your goals and strategies to specific times. Determine what you want to achieve this year, and what you must do to make that happen, and the same for next year, and then for the next few years.

This is your master plan.

In effect, we have arrived at the beginning, back to where we started in the first chapter of this book, back to setting goals and time blocking, and planning your daily, weekly, and monthly schedule. Doing this religiously will be the foundation of your success.

Use this book. Do not put it on the shelf and forget what you have learned. Apply the information you have learned. Make the changes to your current habits that will carry you to success.

CHAPTER 17

CONQUERING YOUR FEAR

Many good residential agents dream of making it in commercial/investment real estate. Some of them take steps to make those dreams come true. They attend training classes and actively seek listings. But for many people, that's where it ends. Something stops those people from turning their dreams into reality.

No matter how you label it—procrastination, too many insecurities, lack of confidence—when you come right down to it, the thing that stops people is fear.

But you do not need to let your plans go by the wayside. You do not need to be afraid to do what it takes to be successful, to step into a new world where you can live the life you want.

With education and the help of coaches and mentors along the way, you can conquer your fears. You can step forward and take advantage of the opportunities for serving clients and making money in the commercial/investment world.

I am here to coach you. The first secret I want to tell you is that you need to show up. You need to show up and use the skills you are learning, and by doing that you can realize your dreams.

There is real money out there, and it is available to you. Step forward, and success will happen for you and your family.

Now, get to it!

CHAPTER 18

FINAL THOUGHTS

I want to leave you with a final thought. Most of my success with commercial/investment sales has come from helping people achieve their goals faster using real estate investment planning strategies.

You can learn some basics, like how to calculate value, return on investment, debt coverage ratio, and so on, facts you will use when selling commercial/investment real estate. But I can tell you that what has helped me more than anything is I have learned how to use these factors to help people get clarity around what they are trying to achieve. I can help them achieve their goals faster by helping them develop written real estate plans and specific strategies that I teach and coach on.

For those of you reading this book who have taken my training courses, either online or in person, you know what I am referring to. When I discuss these things in my future books, I will give more in-depth information about some of the strategies.

Years ago, I realized the need for training, consulting, and coaching, and specifically for the residential real estate agent who wants to add commercial/investment services to their portfolio and merge into the commercial investment real estate arena.

I am here to help you if that is your goal. The ideal way to do that is for you to take training classes, one day or three- day classes, either live or online, so I can share the basic strategies and mindset. I also do coaching and have helped thousands of people succeed at all levels from beginning to intermediate to advanced, and I want to help you succeed as well.

You are welcome to visit my website www.TheNCREA.com, anytime and attend courses, and to reach out to me anytime. I am willing to help you as much as I can through these vehicles.

Thank you for taking the time to read this book. I hope it has been valuable for you. It is the first book for me. To be honest, it has not been one of the easier things I have done. It is difficult for me to slow down and spend time writing, but I am going to get better at it and do more books in the future.

I hope you will share the information here with your friends, and I sincerely hope it will help you achieve your goals. I wish you nothing but continued success.

ABOUT THE AUTHOR

The leading authority in Resimercial Real Estate for 30+ years, Michael Simpson is the Founder and Senior Instructor of The National Commercial Real Estate Association (The NCREA) and is a nationally recognized expert in Commercial Real Estate sales & leasing. Michael and his company are responsible for producing many multi-million dollar producers in the industry.

He enjoys the distinction of being named as one of the Top 1% of agents in the U.S. and one of the Top 3 Commercial Brokers in California and Hawaii. Throughout his career, he consistently closed 50-100 transactions per year, and he is an owner of a brokerage with 250 agents.

Michael's credentials also include:

- *Certified Consultant (C.I.C)*
- *Certified Real Estate Investment Planning Specialist (C.R.E.I.P.S.)*
- *National Commercial Real Estate Advisor (N.C.R.E.A.)*
- *Past Director and Arbitrator for Pacific West Association of Realtors (PWR) 5th largest board in the nation*
- *Past Director & Arbitrator California Association of Realtors (C.A.R.)*
- *REO & Short Sales Specialist*
- *Commercial REO & Short Sale 101 and 102*

When Michael is not teaching real estate agents and brokers how to take over the commercial real estate market, which is one of his true passions, he can be found spending time with his family or enjoying underwater diving and volunteering at the Aquarium of the Pacific. Michael resides in Rossmoor, CA, with his beautiful wife, Angie.

For booking or media inquiries, contact:

Michael Simpson

 www.TheNCREA.com

 info@TheNCREA.com

 877-877-1543

Your one-stop resource for:

- ✓ *One-on-One Coaching*
- ✓ *Group Coaching*
- ✓ *Online Courses*
- ✓ *Seminars and Workshops*
- ✓ *Training & Licensing Agreements for your*
- ✓ *Brokerage*
- ✓ *Monthly & Annual Programs*
- ✓ *Free Courses & More*

Visit www.TheNCREA.com

Looking for direction? Need a clear path to help you achieve your goals?

Request a complimentary **One-on-One Consultation** with one of **our experts.**

www.TheNCREA.com/Request-a-Consultation

Can you talk the talk?

If you met an investor today, are you prepared to have the conversation?

Get your copy of The Ultimate Guide to List & Sell Commercial Investment Property Companion Guide today!

Chocked full of formulas, terminology, scripts and more. Everything you need to understand the basics of commercial real estate.

Available at: